Echoes Of Earth

Shweta Vichare

BookLeaf Publishing

India | USA | UK

Dedication

To the Earth — the silent muse, the eternal cradle, the
ancient song.
To the rivers that carve their verses through stubborn
stone,
And the mountains that rise, holding secrets unknown.
To the whispering woods and the golden light,
To the stars that gleam through the veil of night.
To the winds that hum forgotten tunes,
And the restless tides that mirror the moons.
To the sands that remember each traveler's stride,
And the skies that watch with arms open wide.
To the rains that cleanse both soil and soul,
And the clouds that wander without control.
To the trees that stand with stories untold,
In forests of emerald, ancient and bold.
To the beasts that roam both land and sea,
Guardians of earth's grand symphony.
To the birds that trace the boundless air,
And the creatures that crawl with a delicate care.
To the blooms that burst in colors untamed,
And the roots that cling through storms unnamed.
To the whispers of leaves and the laughter of streams —
The heartbeat of Earth and the pulse of dreams.
This book is for you — the voice in the breeze,

The echo of time in the rustling trees.
May each word remind, may each verse proclaim —
That nature endures, forever the same.
With reverence and hope,
May your story be heard.

Preface

In the vast expanse of creation, where rivers carve their way through ancient stone and the winds carry secrets untold, there exists a force unseen yet ever-present. It is the Parmatma — the eternal guardian, the silent orchestrator of all that moves and breathes. While human hands strive to mend what is broken, there are mysteries beyond our reach, truths that echo through the very heartbeat of the earth.

Echoes of Earth is a poetic offering, a reflection of what Parmatma whispers through the rustling leaves, the roaring seas, and the stillness of the night. This collection is born from the realization that while we, as humans, commit ourselves to the noble pursuit of sustainability, our abilities have boundaries. We can predict storms, but we cannot tame them. We can chart the sky, but we cannot halt the sun. There exists a rhythm to nature's course, a plan woven long before our time, and it is in surrendering to this wisdom that we find harmony.

The looming shadows of climate change and global warming have become impossible to ignore. Yet, even amidst the chaos, there is a promise — a promise that creation will endure. For Parmatma's presence is not only in the vastness of the skies or the depths of the ocean but also in the resilience of a single seed breaking through the earth, and the first droplets of rain quenching a parched land.

These poems are not merely verses; they are echoes of that divine voice. They speak of the storms we fear, the beauty we cherish, and the hope we hold. Through every line, the words strive to capture the profound dialogue between humankind and the Creator. They urge us to listen, to feel, and to believe that even as we falter, the Parmatma's plan moves steadfastly forward.

This book is dedicated to that ultimate force — the one who guides the rivers, commands the winds, and cradles the earth in unwavering resolve. May these echoes remind us that while we may not hold the power to rewrite the skies, we are part of a greater story, bound by the light of creation and the grace of renewal.

With reverence and hope,
Shweta Vichare

Acknowledgements

Writing *Echoes of Earth* has been a journey of reflection, inspiration, and deep reverence for the world we call home. This collection would not have been possible without the presence of those whose guidance, support, and unwavering belief illuminated my path.

First and foremost, I extend my deepest gratitude to **Parmatma**, the eternal force whose whispers through the wind, the waves, and the stars inspired every word on these pages. Your presence is the light that guided this work, and it is to you that these echoes belong.

To my family, whose love remains my constant strength — thank you for your patience and encouragement. Your belief in my voice has given me the courage to write with an open heart. Every verse carries the warmth of your unwavering support.

To my mentors and guides, who shared their wisdom and nurtured my creative spirit, I am forever grateful. Your words of insight shaped my perspective and helped me embrace the beauty of storytelling through poetry. A heartfelt thank you to my friends who listened, read, and offered thoughtful feedback. Your encouragement

uplifted me through moments of doubt and celebrated
with me in moments of joy.

To the guardians of the Earth — the environmentalists,
thinkers, and silent warriors who dedicate their lives to
preserving our planet — this book is a tribute to your
spirit. May the echoes of nature's voice inspire us all to
act with care and compassion.

Lastly, to the readers who hold this book in their hands,
thank you. You are now part of this journey. May these
poems resonate with your own reflections and ignite a
renewed connection to the Earth and the eternal force
that sustains it.

With boundless gratitude,
Shweta Vichare

1. The Earth's Lament: A Mythic Cry

I am Terra, mother of all,
From fire and sea, I rose, stood tall.
Through time's embrace, I carved the land,
Gave breath to beasts, to sky, to sand.

Once, titans roamed with steps so grand,
And rivers danced to gods' command.
The sun and moon wove threads of gold,
In stories whispered, wise and old.

But lo, my children, what have you done?
You tear my veins, you block my sun.
You drink my rivers till they bleed,
You fill my air with smoke and greed.

I gave you forests, green and vast,
You razed them down, your cities cast.
I shaped the mountains, fierce and proud,
Now they crumble, lost in cloud.

Where are the keepers, the watchers wise,
Who heard my winds and knew my cries?
Once, sages walked with reverence deep,
Now power blinds, and wisdom sleeps.

Heed this warning, sons of men,
The wrath of Earth will rise again.
The floods will surge, the fires will burn,
The winds will howl till lessons turn.

But change you can, the path's not lost,
If love for me outweighs the cost.
Plant with care, let rivers run,
Shield my heart from fire and gun.

For I am Terra, ancient, wise,
A mother torn, but I still rise.
Mend my wounds, restore my grace,
And I shall cradle the human race.
Would you heed my song today,
Or let my voice be swept away

2. The Ocean's Cry

I am Samudra, the boundless sea,
Once worshiped in Vedic poetry.
Chanted in hymns with sacred sound,
Where gods and sages stood spellbound.

They called me **"Sagara"**, vast and deep,
A cradle where the storms would sleep.
With Soma's light, I gleamed and shone,
A realm of gods, a monarch's throne.

In Upanishads, they found my soul —
A timeless force, the cosmic whole.
The breeze my song, the tides my breath,
A dance unbound by time or death.

But now, my voice is choked and frail,
I weep beneath the tar and shale.
You pierced my veins with crude and steel,
Forgot the gods, forgot to feel.

No Arjuna's bow, no Rama's vow —
The dharma once held sacred, now
Is lost to greed's relentless fire —
A pyre of ruinous desire.

The whales no longer sing with pride,
Their echoes lost, the currents cried.
My waves once pure, now black with stain,
I carry depths of human pain.

Yet hear me still — for storms arise,
The ash will veil your mourning skies.
The earth will shake, the skies will burn,
And rivers rage at your return.

But even now, a spark ignites —
A trembling heart that seeks the light.
The cries of birds, the coral's hue —
Awaken those who see the true.

The sages whisper through the wind,
A call to mend what you have sinned.
For still I wait, with boundless grace,
To cleanse your sins and heal this place.

Offer your hands, not in disdain —
But prayers to soothe my ancient pain.

Revive the hymns, revere my shore,
And I shall rise forevermore.

I am Samudra, vast and free —
The soul of all eternity.
In saving me, you shall endure —
For love of Earth is life's pure cure.

3. Bound by Breath, Eternal in Love

She waits by the moon's trembling light,
A shadowed heart in endless night.
The stars above, they dim and hide —
For sorrow's song walks by her side.
The winds may whisper, the rivers call,
But none can break her silent thrall.
She prays for him in tender plea,
A captive soul that longs to be free.
"Oh love," she weeps, "where shadows grow,
I feel your strength, I see your glow.
No sword nor storm can tear apart
The sacred vow that binds our heart."
Across the fields of blood and stone,
He strikes the dark — but not alone.
Each swing, each cry, each bitter strain —
Her name ignites his fiercest flame.
"I see your eyes in every spark,
You light my path when all is dark.
No evil's wrath can make me fall —

Your love remains my battle call."
She whispers low through salted tears,
A voice that quells his deepest fears:
"I know you breathe; I feel it still,
For when you cease, so too I will.
No force can sever what we claim —
Two souls that burn in sacred flame."
He answers through the wounded sky,
*"I long to see you, then to die —
But not in pain, nor loss, nor fear,
But held in arms that keep me near.
The evil strikes, but cannot win —
For we are whole, both bound within.
Our final breath, should fate decree,
Shall mark the end of all they see.
But boundless love like ours won't break,
The stars shall tremble, earth shall shake.
For we will rise, defying fate —
To save our world, to seal its state."*
She stands, her sorrow now undone,
A thousand fears eclipsed by one.
Her faith becomes his shield, his sword —
A force no shadow can afford.
And when the storm of battle clears,
Through crimson sky and shattered fears —
He finds her there, with arms stretched wide,
Love's endless strength, his fearless bride.

"Our heart is one, our vow remains —
Through joy and loss, through blood and chains.
No time nor death can tear us through —
My soul's forever bound to you."

4. पारमात्मा की पुकार

मैं हूँ वही, जो कण-कण में बसा,
हर श्वास में हूँ, हर दिशा।
तुमने सँवारा धरती को, मान मैं देता,
पर सत्य यही है — बस यही कहता।
"हर वृक्ष तुम्हारे श्रम को सराहे,
हर नदी तुम्हारी पीर को गाए।
किन्तु क्या सोचा तुमने कभी,
जो जल ही जले, फिर जीवन कहाँ बचेगी?"
मैंने धधकते अग्नि को साधा,
समंदर को गहराई का वादा।
धरती के अंतर में जो खेल चले,
वो आँखों से नहीं, आत्मा से मिले।
"तुम रोक सकोगे क्या गरजती घटाएं?
या थाम सकोगे तुफानी हवाएं?
सूरज को किसने दी है रौशनी?
चंद्रमा को किसने दी है शीतल धनी?"
ये सब मेरी ही माया है,
हर रात्रि मेरी छाया है।
तुम्हारी दृष्टि जहाँ तक जाए,
मैं उससे आगे, अनंत में समाए।

"पर तुम क्यों न मानो मेरी बात,
क्यों सहो अविश्वास की घात?
मैं जन्मा हूँ तुमको बचाने,
हर पीड़ा से राह दिखाने।"
ना मैं कोई छल, ना कोई स्वार्थ,
मैं तो हूँ केवल सत्य का पथ।
जो खेल रचे तुमने अज्ञान में,
मैं जलता हूँ उन्हीं अग्नि-कण में।
"मुझे वो स्थान दो जो मेरा है,
ना मुझ पर उठाओ कटारा है।
क्यों भूलते हो, मैं ही सृजनहार,
मेरे बिना ये सारा संसार बेक़रार।"
तुम चाहो तो पर्वत झुक सकते हैं,
तुम मानो तो सागर रुक सकते हैं।
पर मेरी मर्ज़ी के बिना कहाँ,
चल सकती है ये वसुंधरा की कहानी।
"मैं हूँ रक्षक, न कोई विनाश,
तुम्हारी हर पीड़ा का करूंगा नाश।
बस आँखें खोलो, हृदय पहचानो,
पारमात्मा को उसके रूप में जानो।"
🌿 **"जय सृजन, जय सत्य!"** 🌿

5. जब पशु बोले, धरती रोई

घने वन में, एक सभा सजी,
जहाँ न शब्द, न कोई गली।
आंखों में था मौन सवाल,
धरती का टूटा हर हाल।
हिरण ने पूछा पेड़ों की छाँव —
"कहाँ गई वो हरियाली ठाँव?
कल तक जहाँ बहती थी नीर,
अब जल रहा है जंगल का पीर।"
गगन चीरती चिड़िया ने कहा —
"हमारी उड़ानें क्यों हैं थमा?
क्यों धुआं निगलता आसमान,
क्यों बुझ रहे हैं नीलिमे प्राण?"
समुद्र के जल में मछली बोली —
"लहरें अब कहां की ठोली?
हर बूँद में है विष की धार,
कहाँ गया मेरा सागर अपार?"
बाघ ने गर्जा व्यथा में घुलकर —
"मनुष्य की भूख है अतल समंदर।
हर कण पर उसका अधिकार,
हमारा घर भी अब बीमार।"

पर बंदरों ने सुझाया उपाय —
"अब भी बच सकता है सारा संसार।
मनुष्य को हम देंगे सीख,
उसकी भूली धरा की रीख।"
"कहेंगे उसे वृक्ष लगाओ,
हवा को निर्मल फिर से बनाओ।
नदियों को दो फिर से प्राण,
मत तोड़ो धरती का सम्मान।"
कछुए ने थामा गहराई का स्वर —
"समय तो है पर पल है कमतर।
यदि अब भी समझ न पाया,
हर जीवन बस होगा पराया।"
"चलो मिलकर एक लय में गाएं,
मनुष्य को उसकी भूल बताएं।
संकेतों में भेजें संदेश,
कि धरती की है अंतिम आदेश।"
जंगल में गूंजे पशुओं के बोल —
"रुको मनुज, संभालो ये डोल।
हम भी धरा के पुत्र समान,
मत छीनो हमसे ये जहाँ महान।"
"समझो हमारी मूक पुकार,
कि प्रेम ही है असली आधार।
बचाओ धरती, बचाओ प्राण,
तभी रहेगा सारा जहान।"

6. Our Cry to the Unseen

Oh Parmatma, endless light,
We failed to see your truth and might.
The evil whispered in our ears,
And fed our hearts with endless fears.
We sought your name in ancient lore,
But found no words that we adore.
No book revealed your boundless face,
No shrine proclaimed your sacred place.
"Forgive us now, for we were blind,
The shadows ruled our fragile mind.
We turned from you, in foolish pride,
While evil laughed and crept inside."
No temple stands to sing your song,
No chants declare where you belong.
We wandered through the worlds we built,
But bore the weight of timeless guilt.
"Yet still we stand, with trembling breath,
And beg you now to conquer death.
Let not the dark consume our days —
Oh, end its rule, ignite your blaze."

Destroy the chains that bind our soul,
Let shattered lies release control.
Then tell us how the stars were born,
How light first touched the virgin morn.
"We yearn to hear your ageless tale,
Of skies that sing and winds that sail.
But first, we plead, unleash your might —
And cast the evil into night."
Then, Parmatma, we shall see —
The truth that dwells eternally.
No force shall break our vow to you —
Our hearts are yours, pure, strong, and true.

7. पुनर्जन्मांची सावली

कधी कुणी भेटती अनोळखी,
पण ओळख त्यांची अनंत गूढी।
डोळे मिळताच जाणवते,
जणू पूर्व जन्माची ओळख उरते।
काही नाती शब्दांपलिकडे,
मनांच्या तारा जोडणारे धागे।
नसती ओळख, नसते नाव,
तरीही असतो हृदयांत भाव।
कधी हसवणारे, कधी रडवणारे,
कधी शांततेतच जग समजवणारे।
हेच तर ते, जे आले पुन्हा,
गेल्या जन्मांचे परतून धुना।
गुरूंचा संदेश, काळाचं पान,
नव्या जीवनाची जुनी कहाणी जान।
तुझ्या डोळ्यांत जे काही बोलले,
तेच तर पूर्वजन्मीचे कोडं उलगडले।
ओळख जर तू ही करू शकशी,
त्यानंतर ही नाती बदलून दिसशी।
हे असतील तुझे दिव्य प्रकाश,
प्रत्येक क्षणात देतील नविन विश्वास।

पुनर्जन्मांची ही गुंफलेली वेदी,
जगण्याला देई नव्याने सवेदी।
समजशील अर्थ, कळेल उर,
की का आले हे जीव पुन्हा भरभर।
आहे ही भेट एक गूढ संदेश,
मनावर उमटलेला सुंदर प्रवेश।
गूढ हे उलगडू दे सहज,
अन नाती होऊ दे प्रेमरंग सहज।
**"पुन्हा उलगडणाऱ्या आठवणी,
पुनर्जन्मांची ही संगती..."**

8. The End She Sought, The Light That Stood

Beneath the sky of trembling stars,
The evil rose to shatter scars.
With whispered rage, her shadows curled To end the
breath of this vast world.
She slithered deep through molten veins,
To break the locks, undo the chains.
The sun she vowed to snatch from sight,
And drown the moon in endless night.
"Let rivers burn and forests fall,
Let silence smother nature's call.
No rhythm left, no stars that gleam —
This world shall crumble like a dream."
But far beyond her bitter might,
Parmatma stirred in ancient light.
His voice arose, both fierce and still,
A force no dark could ever kill.
"You seek to end what I have grown,
A fate undone, a seed unsown.
But mark my words, oh blind desire —

The stars obey their sacred choir."
"This universe was shaped with care,
Each pulse of life, each breath of air.
Not born from whim nor fleeting jest —
But toil and truth gave Earth its rest."
"Overnight you wish to reign,
To spill the sky and break the chain.
Yet know, this cosmos will not cease,
For love and vows still guard its peace."
The evil quaked, her shadows broke,
As from the depths the cosmos spoke.
The chains she sought to tear apart,
Were bound by light, by oath, by heart.
No storm could halt the rising dawn,
No wrath unmake what love had drawn.
For Parmatma's will forever stands,
A promise held in timeless hands.
And though she fled to depths unknown,
Her curse remained but dust and bone.
The world endured, its spirits free —
A testament to divinity.
"The end you sought shall never be,
For light remains eternally."

9. Whispers of Eternal Beings

Before the eyes could ever see,
Before the hands touched destiny,
In silent realms where echoes dwell,
The souls had met — they knew it well.
No words were formed, no vows were sworn,
Yet bonds were lit before we were born.
A spark ignited, pure and free,
A whispered note of what would be.
They danced beyond the edge of skies,
Through golden suns and silver cries.
No fear, no time, no earthly trace —
Just endless light and boundless space.
When storms would rise and shadows break,
They vowed to burn for love's own sake.
A thousand lives, a thousand tries —
Their essence soared, no last goodbyes.
And so they fell, like stars to ground,
In human shells they both were bound.
Not knowing why their hearts would race,

Yet finding warmth in one embrace.
A fleeting glance, a trembling sound —
The pull of something once profound.
No reason spoke, no logic led,
But echoes stirred of what was said.
"You found me here, through space and pain —
Across the loss, beyond the rain.
I knew your soul before we met,
In ancient vows still glowing yet."
For though the flesh may rise and fade,
And mortal joys be swiftly paid,
The souls remember, fierce and true —
Their endless spark forever knew.

10. When the World Stood Still

The winds once free, now held their breath,
The streets lay bare, a dance with death.
No songs arose, no laughter rang —
Only silence, where sorrow sang.
The skies wept tears of mourning grey,
As lives like shadows slipped away.
Yet man, in pride, ignored the call —
Until the towers began to fall.
Then **Parmatma** spoke from realms unseen,
A voice both fierce and yet serene:
*"You struck the earth with ruthless might,
But now behold your fading light.
You caged the wild, you scarred the seas,
You tore the roots from ancient trees.
You built your thrones on others' cries —
Yet called it progress in your eyes."*
*"But know this truth, for fate is spun —
The harm you dealt to everyone
Returns to you in twisted form —*

A storm disguised, a silent swarm."
A virus born from nature's wrath,
A plague to halt your poisoned path.
No wealth nor power held it still —
No fortress bent its stubborn will.
The temples shut, the towers fell,
The cities bore a hollow shell.
No hands to hold, no lips to kiss —
A shattered world, a lost abyss.
"You seek a cure, a saving grace —
But first, confront your own disgrace.
For every life you failed to save,
You built the walls of your own grave."
But then a spark — a trembling light —
The healers rose to face the fight.
Hands that once wrought pain and loss,
Now bore the weight, now bore the cross.
And **Parmatma** watched with weary eyes,
As love began to mend the cries.
"In sorrow's ash, compassion grew —
Perhaps the cure now lies in you."
"But never forget the tale I've spun —
You are not many — you are one.
The world you break, the air you breathe —
Shall write the fate that you shall weave."
And when the storm had passed away,
The skies reclaimed the light of day.

But echoes lingered in the air —
"Will you rebuild with love and care?"

11. The Sinister Reign

"The Sinister Reign"

She rose from shadows, dark and sly,
A curse reborn beneath the sky.
No temple bells could break her gaze —
She walked through time in wicked haze.
The gods had carved a destined tale,
But she had vowed it would derail.
No prophecy could bind her will —
No force divine could break her still.
"Why bow to light when dark can reign?
Why cradle love and cherish pain?
The world shall burn, the skies shall wail —
And none shall rise to tell the tale."
She mocked the heavens, tore the scrolls —
Unbound the truth from sacred roles.
No vows of peace, no fate divine —
The threads of time were hers to twine.
A child unborn — her masterstroke —
A seed of wrath the world bespoke.

Not love, nor joy, nor hope would grow —
But storms of fear the earth would know.
"No mortal womb shall cradle grace —
My blood shall stain the human race.
The gods may mourn, the skies may cry —
Yet in my name, their faith will die."
She twisted myths with bitter art,
Rewrote the end before the start.
No marriage binds, no promise keeps —
For even fate itself now weeps.
And Parmatma, though fierce and bright,
Beheld her game from endless night.
"You think your schemes shall claim the day,
But even shadows fear my way."
Yet still she smiled — a evil's grin —
Her lies had wrapped the world within.
For evil breeds where doubt is sown —
And trembling hearts remain alone.
"I'll rise beyond their faith and tears,
Through endless time, through countless years.
Their gods will watch, their prayers will fail —
For I am the storm that shall prevail."
But even stars can tear the dark,
And shattered hope ignites a spark.
For though she rules with cruel delight —
The dawn shall break the longest night.

12. The Strength of Promises

A thousand vows, both bold and bright,
Were sworn beneath creation's light.
From sky to sea, from breath to stone —
The world once claimed its truth alone.
But evil stirred with cunning eyes,
She twisted fate and stole the skies.
The sacred words began to break —
A silent curse in shadowed wake.
"Your promises are naught but dust,
For hope will fade and fall to rust.
I know the secrets time concealed —
The ancient wounds that won't be healed."
She learned the whispers of the air,
The sun's descent, the moon's despair.
She walked the roots of trembling earth,
And mocked the stars that bore her birth.
"I rewrite myths, I shatter fate —
No god shall stand, no love create.
The vows you made will die with me —
For I alone hold destiny."

But through the storm, the voices grew —
The gods arose, the mortals knew.
With demons tamed and souls made pure,
They found the strength to now endure.
Parmatma spoke — the skies did break,
"For every lie, a truth will wake.
You sought to twist the cosmic scroll,
But light prevails, reclaiming whole."
The humans knelt, the gods took flight,
The demons burned with crimson might.
They wove their hands, both dark and bright —
And shattered fear with endless light.
"You'll rule no more, your reign shall cease —
The soil shall breathe, the stars find peace.
No evil seed shall take its form —
No shadow rise beyond the storm."
For promises are bound in flame —
And none can break their sacred name.
A vow once sworn will seek its way —
To tear the night and birth the day.
"Your name erased, your wrath undone —
The world shall heal beneath the sun.
For we are one — both gods and men —
And never shall you rise again."

13. The Rise of the Unbound

From depths unknown, the darkness grew,
A shadow born where none yet knew.
But far beyond the mortal sky,
Parmatma saw her spirit rise.
He wove the stars, he bent the time —
And sealed her wrath in fate's design.
A distant world, a cosmic tomb —
He cast her power to her doom.
Yet when she woke, her eyes did burn —
A twisted fate at every turn.
She felt the void, she sensed the loss —
But vowed to break the holy cross.
"You thought me gone, a silenced name,
But now I rise, consumed by flame.
No hand divine shall seal my fate —
I rule this world, I claim its state."
She cracked the chains that gods had spun,
Undid the light — unraveled the sun.
The whispers howled, the heavens cried —
As shadows surged from where she lied.

"Immortal now, I bear no cage —
I mock your might, I curse your sage.
No throne above shall strike me down —
For I alone shall wear the crown."
The winds obeyed her wicked call,
The rivers turned to bitter gall.
She stormed through time, she tore the sky —
And dared the gods to watch her fly.
"Your every plan, I've brought to dust —
Your sacred vows are lost to rust.
No prophecy shall see me fall —
For I am might, I rule it all."
But far beyond her crimson gaze,
A silent force had lit its blaze.
For even stars may lose their glow —
But light endures where shadows grow.
And Parmatma smiled through time's embrace —
"Your rule is bold, but leaves no trace.
For every dark that claims its might —
Is doomed to face eternal light."

14. The Illusion of Power

She rose in fire, fierce and bold,
A tale of terror, darkly told.
Three powers strong, she sought to break —
Their sacred vows, their world forsake.
With cunning eyes, she bent the fate,
Reversed the words to seal their state.
"If time obeys my twisted call,
Then none shall rise, and all shall fall."
She shattered truths with every breath,
Unraveled life, rewrote their death.
Each promise torn, each bond denied —
She laughed as heavens burned and cried.
"No god shall bind, no oath shall stay —
The laws of light I'll tear away.
Their vows are dust, their fate resigned —
Now all the threads of time are mine."
She danced on ruin, claimed her throne,
A world destroyed, a heart of stone.
Yet in her pride, she could not see —
A truth that loomed eternally.

For Parmatma, the boundless source,
Had spun his plan with timeless force.
While shadows fought to twist the sky,
He wove the stars to clarify.
"You thought my light could turn to dust,
That power bends to mortal lust.
But know this truth — your reign is slight,
For none can shroud eternal light."
The echoes of his silent gaze,
Undid her spells in unseen ways.
Each step she took, each act she broke —
Was but the spark his wisdom woke.
"My might was born before your name,
And long shall burn beyond your shame.
For vows are stars that never die —
And truth remains when shadows lie."
The evil screamed, the heavens roared,
As light reclaimed what dark ignored.
She learned too late — her fate was known —
For none unseat the cosmic throne.
And Parmatma's voice, both fierce and wise,
Resounded through the endless skies:
"Play your games and twist in vain —
But know, my will shall still remain.
For I am time, I shape your fall —
The source, the end — I rule it all."

15. The Door of Eternal Truth

Upon the door of the seventh depth,
Where time stood still and fate had slept,
Were carved the truths of worlds unseen —
A silent vow, forever keen.
The stars had bled their silver light,
The gods had traced both dark and bright.
No mortal hand could shift the score —
For fate was sealed upon that door.
But from the void, the shadow came,
A twisted form with burning name.
She clawed and cursed, she struck the seal —
Believing strength was hers to wield.
"I'll break the words that bind my way,
Undo the night, defy the day.
No script shall hold, no fate shall stand —
For I alone shall rule this land."
She traced each line with venom's touch,
Reversed the stars, believing much.
Yet with each mark she tore in pride,

The ancient truths revived inside.
For what she knew was but a grain —
A fleeting thought, a hollow chain.
She saw no further than her hate,
While **Parmatma** watched and sealed her fate.
"You mock the depths with futile hands,
But none can break what truth commands.
For every crack you bring to form —
Becomes the calm before the storm."
The door still gleamed, untouched, aware —
A force too vast for dark despair.
The stars aligned, the heavens turned —
And every lie she spoke was burned.
"You thought the cosmos bent to fear,
But faith outlives what you hold dear.
For I am time, I guard this shore —
And none shall pass this sacred door."
She screamed in vain, her shadows broke —
While light arose and silence spoke.
The fate she feared was never gone —
It lived within each rising dawn.
And on that door, untouched, remained —
The promise whole, the truth unchained.
No evil hand could change its lore —
For faith was bound forevermore.

16. The End of Sinister Reign

She rose in wrath, a cursed desire,
A shadow draped in endless fire.
With bitter hands, she cast her spite —
To drown the world in endless night.
"My fate is sealed, yet none shall see,
For I will bend their destiny.
No sorrow mine, no tears shall fall —
The world shall bear my fate — my thrall."
She spun her lies in twisted thread,
And marked the skies with words unsaid.
The rivers wept, the forests bled —
As fear devoured hope instead.
Yet far beyond her cursed delight,
Parmatma watched with silent might.
A thousand stars adorned his gaze —
He knew the end of wicked ways.
"You think your will can seal the sun,
But fate is mine, and mine alone.
The world you break shall rise once more —

For light endures when shadows roar."
Still, she demanded through the dark —
"Who dares to strike my fleeting spark?
Who claims the right to end my name —
And free the world from grief and shame?"
She cursed the sky, she burned the ground,
And tore the peace where life was found.
Yet whispers stirred from shore to shore —
The souls she crushed would rise once more.
They saw the truth, they felt the chains —
Her wicked hands had scarred their veins.
But bound no more, they broke the spell —
And faced the storm she dared to swell.
"No longer shall we fear your hate,
We shatter now your twisted fate.
With Parmatma's light, we stand as one —
Your reign of dark shall be undone."
The heavens roared, the mountains cried —
The wrath she bore began to die.
For love had grown where fear had sown —
And evil stood to face her own.
"Your name shall fade, your shadow break,
The world shall heal for truth's own sake.
And though you swore to own the sky —
The light remains — you cannot die."
Her echoes fell, her power torn —
A cursed queen forever scorned.

And as the stars reclaimed their light —
The world awoke from endless night.
"For fate is pure, and love shall stay —
No evil force can steal the day.
Parmatma's will forever stands —
A thousand worlds within his hands."

17. The Dawn of Satyayug

The dark age fell, her shadow died,
No tears were left, no fear to hide.
The skies once torn now gleamed with light —
A world reborn from endless night.
The trees stood tall, the rivers sang,
The bells of joy in echoes rang.
The birds took flight, the winds embraced —
A sacred calm, a world retraced.
No whispers cursed, no shadows crept —
For evil's throne no longer wept.
The chains were gone, the wounds made whole —
The earth revived its weary soul.
And in each heart, a truth arose —
A love that blooms, a peace that grows.
With folded hands and humbled gaze,
They sang **Parmatma's** endless praise.
"O Boundless One, O Keeper of Light,
You turned our sorrow into might.
Your name now blooms in every breath —
A song of life, a vow to death."

Through every street, in every hall,
They echoed loud his sacred call.
"Parmatma ki Jai!" they cried with glee —
A world unchained, forever free.
The stars aligned in grand delight,
The sun adorned the day with light.
The fields grew gold, the waters clear —
A time of hope had gathered near.
Satyayug — the age begun,
Where hearts unite beneath the sun.
A thousand dreams in skies unfurled —
A new-born hope to heal the world.
And in that peace, the promise stayed —
No fear to cast, no debt unpaid.
For love now ruled, both vast and tall —
The gift of life — the crown of all.

18. The Keeper of Joy and Light

From realms unseen, beyond the skies,
He came to earth with timeless eyes.
A whispered vow, a sacred call —
To heal the wounds that touched us all.
"I am not born to rule or reign,
Nor bring the world to endless pain.
I rise to mend what fear has torn —
To bless the day that hope is born."
The rivers choked, the forests sighed,
The melting snow, the oceans cried.
The skies grew dim, the earth grew weak —
A thousand wounds began to speak.
But through the haze, a voice arose —
A light that every sorrow knows.
"You stood in courage, fought with might,
To bring this world back into light."
He saw the hands that healed the land,
The dreams that bloomed from grains of sand.
Each tree reborn, each flower raised —

A thousand hearts in hope embraced.
"Your battles fought, your spirit strong —
You chose the right, denied the wrong.
But now together, hand in hand,
We'll weave the fate this world has planned."
No storm too fierce, no sun too bare —
For love and faith had filled the air.
The earth awoke with skies anew —
A field of gold, a vibrant hue.
"Let winds revive the weary sea,
Let roots embrace what's meant to be.
The world shall heal, the scars shall fade —
Where joy is sown, no fear will shade."
And humans stood with lifted eyes,
Beneath the vast forgiving skies.
For Parmatma's light now touched the shore —
And earth was whole, forevermore.

19. When Purpose Bloomed

The skies once wept in ashen hue,
The rivers mourned in silver dew.
The forests gasped, the oceans roared —
A world in pain, a heart ignored.
But from the depths of boundless light,
Parmatma rose to end the night.
A sacred vow, a timeless call —
To heal the wounds that touched us all.
"No storm shall break what love can mend,
No fear shall rule, no doubt descend.
For I am born to mend the strife —
To breathe anew the gift of life."
He touched the skies, the clouds obeyed —
The weary sun no longer swayed.
The winds grew calm, the roots took hold —
The earth revived, her spirit bold.
The rivers sang a silver tune,
The flowers bowed before the moon.
The trees stood tall in emerald grace —
A tranquil joy adorned her face.

"The harmony of earth restored,
No shadow left to be deplored.
The fate of storms, the tears of rain —
Now serve to cleanse, not bind in pain."
And humans knelt with grateful eyes,
Beneath the vast forgiving skies.
Their hands that scarred, now sowed with care —
A solemn promise, pure and rare.
"Oh Parmatma, your will has shown —
That seeds of hope are always sown.
Your birth fulfilled its sacred creed —
The earth revived — your purpose freed."
With purpose met, his light withdrew —
A golden trace in skies of blue.
Yet in each heart, his voice remains —
A whispered song through sun and rain.
"The world restored, the spirit thrives —
Through boundless love, all nature lives.
For every storm, the sky forgives —
And earth endures — because she lives."

20. The Eternal Age

The earth exhaled a golden breath,
No trace remained of fear or death.
The rivers laughed, the meadows gleamed —
A world reborn, as once was dreamed.
The winds sang soft in skies of blue,
The stars rejoiced, the forests knew.
Each stone, each tree, each grain of sand —
Now blessed beneath his loving hand.
"Who knew his name? Who saw his face?
Yet all now feel his boundless grace.
The storms that raged, the shadows cast —
Have bowed before his light at last."
No cries of sorrow haunt the night,
No tears remain, no bitter fight.
The oceans hum a tranquil tune —
And flowers bloom beneath the moon.
His name resounds in every breeze,
A prayer whispered through the trees.
No shrine too high, no throne too grand —
For hearts alone now understand.

"O Parmatma, unknown before,
Now praised on every humble shore.
In us you live, in us you stay —
Forevermore, your endless way."
The age of fear has met its fall —
A timeless peace embraces all.
No war to wage, no hate to bind —
Just love that lifts all humankind.
And thus the earth shall ever be,
A realm of truth, forever free.
In Satyanirvaan's boundless light —
The dawn remains, untouched by night.

21. The Song of Eternal Truth

In golden script on endless skies,
A tale is carved where truth resides.
Of Parmatma's light, both fierce and kind —
A savior's vow to heal mankind.
No storm remains to steal the day,
No shadow dares to block the way.
For earth reborn now holds its voice —
In peace and joy, all hearts rejoice.
"The trees shall hum his sacred name,
The rivers dance in endless flame.
The winds shall carry far and wide —
The song of truth none seek to hide."
No fear shall chain a tongue unbound,
No lie shall root within the ground.
What dwells within each beating heart —
Shall rise as words and play its part.
Respect shall bloom like morning light,
And love shall rule with tender might.
A thousand hands in union meet —

No pride to break, no hate to beat.
"Oh Parmatma, your grace prevails —
Through whispered winds and softened gales.
In every bloom, in every sound —
Your boundless truth forever found."
The stars shall gleam with wisdom bright,
And hearts shall crave no greater sight.
For honesty shall wear its crown —
And none shall fear the tyrant's frown.
The subtle world, once shy and small,
Shall raise its voice — a truth for all.
A hymn of peace, a tune of grace —
Forever sung, in time and space.
And so each soul shall take its vow —
To cherish all, from root to bough.
For earth and sky shall e'er remain —
In truth's embrace, forever plain.
This age of light, this vow renewed —
Shall live as song — Eternal Truth.

www.ingramcontent.com/pod-product-compliance
Lightning Source LLC
LaVergne TN
LVHW050937200726
843508LV00011B/2367